21st Century
Basic Skills
Library

BABY ZOO ANIMALS
KOALA BEARS

by Katie Marsico

Cherry Lake Publishing • Ann Arbor, Michigan

3

CHERRY
LAKE
Publishing

Published in the United States of America
by Cherry Lake Publishing
Ann Arbor, Michigan
www.cherrylakepublishing.com

Content Adviser: Dr. Stephen S. Ditchkoff, Professor of Wildlife Sciences,
Auburn University, Auburn, Alabama

Photo Credits: Cover and page 1, ©Keith Wheatley/Shutterstock, Inc.;
page 4, ©Andras Deak/Dreamstime.com; page 6, ©tbkmedia.de/Alamy;
page 8, ©BMCL/Shutterstock, Inc.; page 10, ©covenant/Shutterstock, Inc.;
page 12, ©Zepherwind/Dreamstime.com; page 14, ©Keith Wheatley/
Dreamstime.com; page 16, ©Hotshotsworldwide/Dreamstime.com;
page 18, ©Ben Mcleish/Dreamstime.com; page 20, ©ASSOCIATED PRESS

Library of Congress Cataloging-in-Publication Data
Marsico, Katie, 1980–
  Koala bears / by Katie Marsico.
      p. cm. — (21st century basic skills library) (Baby zoo animals)
  Includes bibliographical references and index.
  ISBN 978-1-61080-457-8 (lib. bdg.) — ISBN 978-1-61080-544-5 (e-book) —
ISBN 978-1-61080-631-2 (pbk.)
1. Koala—Infancy—Juvenile literature. 2. Zoo animals—Infancy—
Juvenile literature. I. Title.
  SF408.6.K52M37 2013
  599.2'5—dc23   2012001728

Cherry Lake Publishing would like to acknowledge
the work of The Partnership for 21st Century Skills.
Please visit *www.21stcenturyskills.org* for more information.

Printed in the United States of America
Corporate Graphics Inc.
July 2012
CLFA11

TABLE OF CONTENTS

Not Really Baby Bears

Koala bears are not actually bears at all. They are **marsupials**!

Koalas are found in eastern Australia.

They also live in zoos around the world.

Koalas have one **joey** at a time.

Baby koalas are hairless and blind when they are born.

They look a little like pink jelly beans!

A joey climbs into its mother's pouch after being born.

It stays there for about 6 to 7 months.

A Koala's Day

Baby koalas spend most of their time sleeping.

Adults do, too.

Koalas often nap for up to 18 hours a day!

Adult koalas eat **eucalyptus** leaves.

A joey drinks its mother's milk. This continues for the first 6 months of its life.

A joey stays close to its mother. This is true even after it leaves her pouch.

The joey rides on her belly or back.

Zookeepers hear joeys and their mothers **communicate**.

The koalas make noises called bellows. A bellow sounds like a snore followed by a belch.

Leaving Mama Marsupial

Joeys learn to eat eucalyptus leaves and live by themselves.

They leave their mothers after about 1 year.

Female koalas are adults when they are about 3 years old. Then they can start having joeys of their own.

Then there are new koalas at the zoo!

Find Out More

BOOK

Clark, Willow. *Koalas*. New York: PowerKids Press, 2012.

WEB SITE

National Geographic Kids—Koalas
*http://kids.nationalgeographic.com/kids/animals/
creaturefeature/koala*
View a video about koalas and send a koala e-card.

Glossary

communicate (kuh-MYOO-ni-kate) share information, ideas, or feelings

eucalyptus (yoo-kuh-LIP-tuhs) a fast-growing evergreen tree found in Australia and nearby Pacific islands

joey (JOH-ee) a baby koala

koala bears (koh-AH-luh BAYRS) small, bearlike marsupials that live in Australia

marsupials (mar-SOO-pee-uhlz) mammals that feed and carry their young in pouches

zookeepers (ZOO-kee-purz) workers who take care of animals at zoos

Home and School Connection

Use this list of words from the book to help your child become a better reader. Word games and writing activities can help beginning readers reinforce literacy skills.

a	bellows	followed	learn	new	the
about	belly	for	leave	noises	their
actually	blind	found	leaves	not	themselves
adult	born	hairless	leaving	of	then
adults	by	have	life	often	there
after	called	having	like	old	they
all	can	hear	little	on	this
also	climbs	her	live	one	time
and	close	hours	look	or	to
are	communicate	in	make	own	too
around	continues	into	mama	pink	true
at	day	is	marsupial	pouch	up
Australia	do	it	marsupials	really	when
baby	drinks	its	milk	rides	world
back	eastern	jelly	months	sleeping	year
beans	eat	joey	most	snore	years
bears	eucalyptus	joeys	mother	sounds	zoo
being	even	koala	mother's	spend	zookeepers
belch	female	koala's	mothers	start	zoos
bellow	first	koalas	nap	stays	

Fast Facts

Habitat: Forests
Range: Eastern Australia
Average Height: 23.5 to 33.5 inches (60 to 85 centimeters)
Average Weight: 20 pounds (9 kilograms)
Life Span: About 20 Years

Index

About the Author

Katie Marsico is the author of more than 100 children's and young-adult reference books. She has already seen koalas at the zoo and would love to watch them in the wild one day in Australia.